Walking Through Ground

Poems of healing in the Peak District and beyond

Elise Freshwater-Blizzard

Walking Through Ground©
Copyright © 2022 By Elise Freshwater-Blizzard

All rights reserved. Printed in the United Kingdom. No part of this book may be used or reproduced in any manner whatsoever without written permission except in the case of brief quotations embodied in critical articles or reviews. This book is a work of fiction. Names, characters, businesses, organisations, places, events and incidents either are the product of the author's imagination or are used fictitiously. Any resemblance to actual persons, living or dead, events or locales is entirely coincidental. Publisher: Independent Publishing Network

Publication Date: September 2022

ISBN: 978-1-80352-118-3

Author: Elise Freshwater-Blizzard

Website: https://www.youtube.com/channel/UCgjxXWWPKMBAxkeXEC1gKkA

Email: elisefreshwaterblizzard@yahoo.co.uk

Youtube: Elise Freshwater Blizzard

Instagram: elisefreshwaterblizzard

Please Direct all enquiries to the author

10 9 8 7 6 5 4 3 2 1

For all the cavers who have known me, and those who helped me grow overground and underground- I am proud of our time together, and can't wait to meet those who will make my journey more vibrant in the future. Our scars are truly a roadmap for others.

A following thank you to those who may have taken or been in any of the photos throughout this book...

and the biggest thank you to the TSG, your members have taught me that caving without compassion, just isn't caving at all.

I.

My cold hard exterior.
$\qquad\qquad\qquad$ *Breaks.*
$\qquad$ *abrases.*
$\qquad\qquad\qquad\qquad$ *from the acid*
$\qquad\qquad\qquad\qquad\qquad$ *upon acid*
that intertwines and fills in my cracks of glistening limestone.
my once thick, hard slab,
runs down with the water, gushing for seconds
and millions of years

$\qquad$ *but one drop has made me succumb to my knees*
$\qquad\qquad$ *to kneel back down under the elements*
$\qquad\qquad\qquad$ *only*
$\qquad\qquad$ *for another million years to*
$\qquad\qquad\qquad\qquad$ *hollow me out, again.*

Peak Cavern in Flood, Summer 2021

Red Flag

Lying in my little tent
snuggled in my sleeping bag
I stare upon the ceiling vent
the walls fly red flags

tent poles quake in mud
back pressed on cold stone
hoping, wishing the tent stays up
and wanting for old days at home

where the fire lit my face up so,
and family gathered round to talk
replaced by a chill into my bones
      and now on a path, alone, I walk.

The Hole in the Ground

Like Ants burrowing under the soil, they accumulate inside the hole. A grey bearded man purposefully peers into the shops, his back arching so slightly, whilst the woman with a red scarf speeds over him with her window, loud, open, course, adventure on top. Two strangers so close, divided by thin road. A young girl gazes up to the racing clouds, collecting her luck in the protection of the wind. A group of young men form ashes and chewing gum on a dark and dusty corner under the roof, marking their territory in the circus around them.

But the needle strikes upon its jaded path, for the shutdown was only too soon into the day. Now I stand upon a complex Sheffield and can only imagine the hole is but still there: deteriorating within solid brick, echoing underground soul.

> [Roll, press and squash this forged iron into rolls of metal fat that bulge out, spilling over onto the edges of the city and pulsate the lines that send fluid into its heart. Gliding past my feet, I curtsey to the ingenious steel that unites these five rivers to the same heart.]

Mirror of the Peak

the wind shreds away this identity
as I walk on the grey
steel city,
that only glints faintly in the dark

abandoning the cold concrete-
for who am I, for just another foot on the path?
(with its neglected chewing gum stuck to my shoe)

and here I have come like many others
another lost soul that has come to sit
to overlook the galloping paradise far away

The Peak District.
We come here all too often.

You, there, sink into your phone,
whilst they, steal kisses in the dark
huddled in their warmth of love
and them, speak in dreary whispers
under influence of cold cans
and hot green wisps that made them forget
about the frozen mass behind them

...like an iceberg over our heads
whilst we sit on the edge of Sheffield.

But our backs are turned.
I inhale the winds of the peak
flowing towards me,
the icy touch burns my skin

I'm not alone when you
reach out and climb down my throat
a friend that won't escape

A dark message you have written ahead:
I must travel to sit in you.
Contemplate you-

to lay upon
your
deep blankets of darkness under your threatening
heights

and deep inside your lungs where moonlight cannot
touch
and just like the water I will always
flow
      back
          to-
                    you.

Ranger

knowing eye that scans his mistress
deciphering her delicate spine.
secret twisting tracks
on burrow of bone
to be wandered and hailed.
hidden villages,
together like jigsaw pieces
on the OS map he crumples.

Vitality pushed out of lungs
hurling mist taking over land,
farmer beginning breakfast
ranger's toll on his caked hands
knowing both that this land is his
and will also never be his
whilst-
knowing he belonged to
her watchful eye
all along

My land of Free

My land of free-
You do not own me
and nor do I own the footsteps I take upon
My land of free.

My land of free-
Wallowing in ev'ry peak
but does not sit still when the sun hits stone
My land of free.

My land of free-
Winnat's pass had hit me
like the rock on my skull against your soft moss
My land of free.

My land of free-
Kinder Scout's calling me
I won't stop walking until I kiss the top
In my land of free-

Stonewall

Millstone Grit

wind. grain. flour. bold.
grind. sacked. brought. sold.
pounded. worked. cut. steel.
produce. millstone. Peak. heal.

thousands. scattered. working. paid
giving. providing. produce. weighed
life. giving. millstone. hit
knives. forks. Sheffield. grit

pivot. grind. progress. mould.
new. wireless. innovate. bold.
inspire. drive. computer. tech.
cars. planes. timeless. forget.

sunken. broken. walked. stone.
timeline. spoken. Stanage. grown.
quarry. millstone. rounded. moss.
abandoned. hidden. hurt. lost.

Spicy Cold Caving

Dear Cavers,

Take comfort that the underground dwells beneath our feet
for no reason other than to be there.
The pointlessness of an unhabitable environment
only favours the beauty of the un-human
The un-destructive
The un-capitalisation.
For who wants to spend long in a chamber of horrors?
Yet I know of men who have.
no man would pay another for such self-destructive practices
of fear
but the caver has seen their own vices far beyond others
they have reached the unhabitable,
felt the glory of dirt between their teeth
and seen the unforgiving drops that would terrorise most
who simply live to try not to die another day
whilst we live more than ever
walking on the face of death
and in the valley of fear.
No man will pay you- but you have payed yourself.

Post-Pandemic

It's been such a while; friend, lover.
I wave at you in the morning.
In the afternoon, you waved back with a soft pink sky in your hands.
I forgot how simple you were.
Seeing your light soft blues
I blushed,
and you blushed back.

Sunrise on Mam Tor

Lady Bower

I'd swim across Lady Bower
with my shoes holding me down-
heavy laces undone
and clothes
swamping past the underwater roofs
of the village beneath
all just to be alone with you.
but instead
I stare across the room
at grey eyes
as they hold someone else's gaze
they turn blue
with someone else's hand
but I simply tell myself
that one day:
I will swim across Lady Bower.

Restful night

slowly turning,
your belly expanding and releasing
mother mountain
I feel your heartbeat pull me in:
sinking head rests on your back
as I fall into peaceful slumber in your hidden curves
d r i p p i n g down round your bones
and forever, you have me.

Access to Peak

Locked, bolted, sealed, permission.
What type of gesture do I need to make?
To kiss your fairest hand under the moonlight sky
and wrap my arms around your tender curves.
I can only stand here and bid you farewell,
under the almighty god, who have you ever in keeping.
But I do request that the next lover that comes your way
is far more noble, steadfast, and worthy of your
wet trenches and folded paths

Strolling back from Gaping Gill

The Kind Caver

Deep where the water rushed low
was where you offered your shoulder for the first time
I stood on it, tall
to lower into your arms.

but high where the dust floats in the mines,
bolted gently, rusted,
you mock my me whilst
my weight is hanging on a thawing bolt.
thinly-layered kindness
under mean intention.
Life, hanging by a thread
Life, hangiand you'd help with a laugh.

A man tends to his children in a bothy, Gaping Gill

Roger Rains, Peak Cavern

Standing on the Shoulders of Giants

The moment I fell back, my body losing all focus
limbs, indistinct
and life,
inching to fatality
was the moment I had begun to live.

THUD and my back was thrown down one step
CRACK as my hips took the force on the next
BLANK as my mind was thrown out of its skull

you, with your witless ways, lunged forward to hold me, to
save me
fear in your voice, but I could not hear
I only heard what was within me
the breath I had soaked within
and the sharp pain upon my back

and in that moment, Giants had sent a clear message,
that the fall would ripple throughout my life as a warning:
a centimetre closer to the edge that wrapped around my
sides
and I would hurtle towards my final moments:
and him:
explaining my wrong decisions, blaming me
whilst dying
alone.
but instead

I lived.
You gave me a chance.

And hobbling out; free, new, and freshly bruised
you told me; my lover, ever so sweetly:

"I could have carried you out in a body bag instead."
and then I knew-
whilst being silenced,
I must re-write my life.

I now stand on the shoulders of Giants

Plato's Cave [ii]

That day, she heard your echoing voice, and at once thought: "I had forgot that I could speak! But daren't under the black pressure wrapped around my tongue." And at once, she had spied a dim blue light flood into the chamber. "Light! Light!" From across the room, her heart elevated as a butterfly would flap its wings: at once slow, but then faster before it takes its flight, perhaps stretching before making its new journey. Slowly clambering her way ahead, a new excitement struck like a match in her heart, igniting blue flame. Her hands and knees did not feel as raw as before, as if to believe that the pale yellow tinge flooding in from across the room had numbed the pain of years of neglect.

Derwent Dam

The unbroken path

It was only until this moment that I realised I had walked the same path: *day in, day out.*
An endless loop that kept me bound to the old dirt: scuffed shoes and worn out bones.
the round-trip walked for decades, with no other way on in sight.
I shone a light and scattered my eyes for a lost path.
I clambered among rocks, dug out old mud that sucks and clogs routes dry.
a way on, a new route
a new life
a new path
let you be unbroken:
let me set you free
so that new legs may walk you and love your cave more tenderly
and I shall name you; 'the unbroken path'
for neglected stone does not harbour hate,
but love and care for your new ways, new connections
new chances,
new love!

I love you, my unbroken path.

The White Beast

Upon the valley is a white cardboard box
which hits the eye like a ton of bricks,
beats the green from the grass
and sucks the blue from the air

Upon the valley there is a grey monster,
with a thousand black square eyes
a paper towel cardboard tube snout
that billows out grey morning clouds

Upon the valley there is a Hope
to a stranger on unrequited land
where a white finger points alone
naked with its pipes and glands

Because upon the Valley I fell in love
with a monster, grey on grey,
he sits and waits for lost souls
guiding them, night and day.

Hope Cement Works in the background

Ghost

The first time I slept in a cave
I was scared of... the beings in the dark
even when I calmed down
they were still there.　　S T I L L 　　T H E R E ...
Was it 10PM?
　　　　　　　　　　　Or 1AM?

Opening and closing my
waste-paper basket eyes
it made no difference:
for there was no light.

Nothing to separate the dusk and dawn.
Nothing to see and nothing to watch.
Just Black upon Black,
uncomfortable Black.
Lucid Black.
Legs and back
against the cold floor
but wrapped and cocooned
caterpillar huddling in secret
vulnerable to the prey
it is blind to.

But then I woke up
And the Black disappeared into my torch
To see that it was 9:30 in the morning,
I had slept in!
the morning was far away from me
because I was still in Black
but this time it was

warm Black.
Glowing Black.
Honey Black.
Relaxed back,
such as man appreciates
the butterfly
I was overseen by the maker
the destroyer.
my love,
I would always show my wings to you!

Filming underground comes with challenges

Orange Cavity

If it wasn't for every biting winter
gnawing on the life of the leaves,
sucking them dry and crunching apart
then there would be no second chances-
I long for those fresh youthful berries
That give me a second chance
to throw away the dry husks in my mind.
rubbing away the old, crusted paint
painting fresh new oils to reveal
an orange juicy scene, foretold,
as the present looks bright, once again

Edale

As the sun sets,
so my heart sinks
for I may not see;
the traveller on his feet
or the local, on the street.

There's a glow on the mountain:
as if fireflies surrounded a tree,
their dim green shine scattered upon the grass.
Those glowing tents resting on Kinder's belly,
giving rest to those souls and their tired feet

reflected down upon the valley,
golden pubs hide in bitter dark-
a brew with a stranger, now a friend.
suddenly, the dark is not so unfamiliar
as the ground is still breathing its old rhymes
and the church lay silent under shaking trees.
the paths that snake the mountain lay to rest

E d a l e   i s   g l o w i n g   o n c e   a g a i n .

Sunrise on Mam Tor

The sunlight pours down into the green and yellow slopes
so my tired eyes can open up
but impossible to open wide enough to ...
...soak the soul in
and see the secrets that the small green trees
might be able to tell

I could imagine the old songs
chiming from Peak Cavern
echoing to the edges Mam Tor
and vibrating in its foundations:
those songs from old
now drifting in the seas of time
floating within a rope-maker's memory
never drifting back to sand.

but new day
floods from horizon
and again we begin:
across the glinting golden farms
within the resting hidden village

I am endlessly thankful
and lucky to rest my eyes upon Castleton
and the tower that broods from Hope
I've fallen in love with
that bumble in the early morning
that rests like the mists upon my old valley.

as cavers rise from cocoons,
they trundle through graves
humming their new songs
of hardships and adventures
to those old rope-makers
as they lie in their sleep

walking through miner's town,
once a home to hundreds,
weaving in cavern deep,
now ticketed at entrance,
and shut by 4 for tea.

Therapist

If the world is in torment for many years
all can be tempered, calmed, and straightened out
by a loving walk on the soft hands of the Peak
holding your feet lightly and encouraging your playful smile.

A Pause to rest your feet

*Could you ever imagine
a place so dreary that your
very eyes cannot see, and yet
eternity is right in front of you?*

Looking for something, perhaps caves

Re-entrance

Tapping away at the earth in this secluded tunnel
Exploring this twisting and turning mind
Slowly shovelling the mud away from my soul
Hauling it out on bucket, piece by piece
For it to be tossed out of the murky depths.

Every cut, graze and sigh causes
clumps of rocks to crumble away from the mud
And sometimes, an explosion
The pain ringing in my ears
And waiting for the dust to settle
As I crouch down to remember the harshness of their words.
I look forward
My meagre light shines on an old chamber I had buried long ago
Thick with my mud of ignorance and denial
Lost, in the corners of my mind
Ready to be explored again

The bottom of P8

Black dust floats round my mind.
If I could soak gold into my lungs, I would.
Here I lie down at the bottom of P8.
I question why my life seems so early.
Or too late.
If I could have learned to breathe in gold
would I still have my sunken, pitted eyes?

but I am but a small water droplet,
 happy we are in the same stream.
Fleetingly we meet,
and part ways with flood,
 so I'll search for you at the bottom of it all.
Knowing you'll take the same journey

Fir St.

warm breath swirling in circles,
dancing round the room
and warming up our hearts.
pillows on laps
fingers tucked between thighs
and legs crunched into chest-
unanticipated love-
sitting in that room
it's now cold
gone
lost
but forever tucked away in my eye

a cavers' secret hub
our little den
food, wine, smiles
huddled round a tv screen
speaking more words than we had all week
parroting over the screen

One day- it will all be lost.
will the house remember our legacy
when the generations have all but gone?
Stories to be untold
lessons, to be unwritten
memories, to be unkept.

….
high up in the attic.
...
the smallest whisper.

at midnight:

my secret of Fir. St.

cool blue fire: burning in my mind.
The secret that lay in front of me all along-
was it hidden in the floorboards I walked upon?
The caving kit caked in the mud of a thousand old trips
filled with young bloods.
The trauma we fought to get here,
travelled so far across the seas of our minds
filled with wakeful tears
to land on our backs,
top bunker:
with morning kisses
in the silent cloud above the memories.
thunder let me stay.

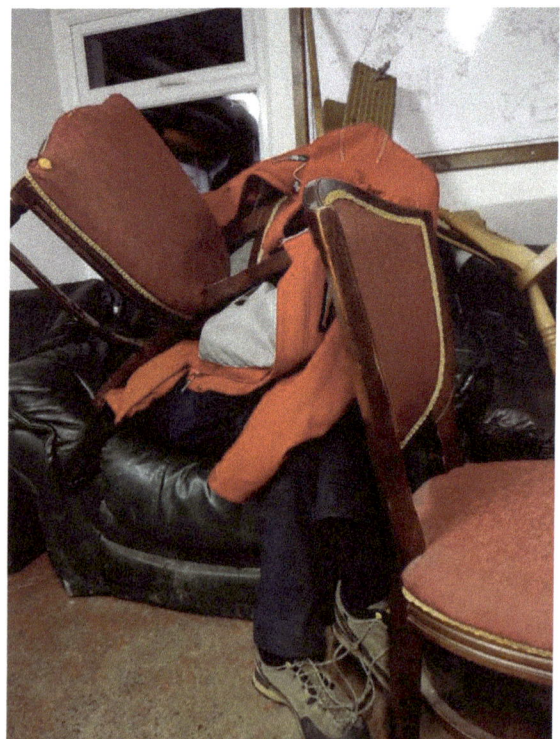

Do NOT fall asleep in a caving hut...

Forgetting you

we turned up each day to mine
shovel
turn over mud
fire into the rock until it crumbled
like sandpaper, rubbing away it's courseness
with thunderous water,
we created new hallways only we knew
and secret rooms that we could share
and then one day I waited for you to show- with no avail.
I kept digging on my own, looking at the now jarred and achy corridors
wondering why I was alone to keep digging.
people from the outside jealous of our lavish entrance,
 when it became a symbol of my own work: where were you?
It used to be everyday,
now once a week you'd pick a shovel up and toss aside a lump of clay
only to walk away and tell me
'my work is done'
There comes a moment where you just have to stop.
digging.

My favourite place in the world, the windy gates (Winnat's Pass)

protection

whatever path you may choose
please don't be afraid
my little bean
for my sturdy arms
and strong heart
looks after you from afar
and breaks down every monster there lies before you

this cave-wall,
is it actually looking at you?
A thousand years have passed
Humanity painted onto stone
I'm sure you don't mean to give me that
cold, hard stare,
because your diamonds are glistening in the night
I thought I was here for you but
you were waiting for me to add my oily touch onto

Prussicking Gaping Gill

Boundless

I prussic high above it all,
Just to be at ground floor
And no matter how high I climb
I'm still beneath the weight of the earth
But poke my head above the floor
and your face beams above
there to hold my hand
after all the hard work was done

Plato's Cave [iii]

The smell of grass was pungent and strong against her face as the mist slowly cleared the way by the exit. It filled her chest and mind so strongly, she had to stay and rest upon the yellow walls to recover from such a beautiful smell. The sweet smell of sheep shit sank into her as the juices of a tea leaf sinks into hot water and her heart felt ablaze with the passion and fury of life. Another inbreath, another drop of oil to lubricate her throat, like cogs that had stiffened over years of neglect, they were finally dusted off and inch by inch, began to creak into movement. She had finally left her cave, ready for another day.

i.

There is nothing as graceful as
a woman,
tugging,
ever so sweetly
at her trousers
to squat down
in the depths of the forest,
or on top of a mountain
to relieve herself on the floor.

Legs, wide over stream
or over cliff
and a man would still
Fall
deeply in love with this charm that only a woman may
leak

sitting down
Half-naked
buttocks pressed against the sweet moss
she laid there
watching the view:
A farmer drives his tractor in a field below,
tourists gaze upon the green tides over yonder.
a boy watches her as small as a grain of sand

as the clouds moved like butter
a smile begins to form
as she jaunts her trousers up
and continues on adventuring,
hair gracefully flying in the wind

men may only seek to find such grace in such a private act

Chatsworth House.

He took my hand at Chatsworth House.
Summer gleaming down on nose
He took my hand at Chatsworth house.
cascading water flows through toes
He took my hand at Chatsworth house.
playful bubble as we stroll
He took my hand at Chatsworth house.
Round the maze and on the knoll.

He took my hand at Chatsworth House
fingered hands soft 'til memory struck.
He took my hand at Chatsworth house;
and let them go as old lover snuck-
he took my hand at Chatsworth house
now I wander for my own sake
because he took my hand at Chatsworth house
and now thinks of hers to take.

The heartbreak of desire

perseverance pot held me by hips
and lips as you pushed your hands round my back
and mine onto yours

and yet,
stuck between a rock and a hard place-
I wish I had kissed you more
and given less.
maybe then, the silt would not have been mixed with
salty tears on my tongue.

those past infected words of betrayal still bound inside that chamber.
Sitting in the space my hips had been.

Present moment

The wind cannot promise to flow into my lungs,
But instead of holding my breath, *I smile*.

Lud's Church

Take a rest, deep under the fresh bleeding cut I own.
Then, walk within the chasms that run thick
as the mud climbs up your shoes, and mist crawls down
your neck

a lone hare fell down my moulded steps one soggy day
startled little legs when choir sang:
and found the devout, gathered deep in hush whispers

voices that hide in thick walls, saturated in moss,
soaking in the torment that the words bring.
but landing softly on the ears of others' tongues

deeply carved face looking out over me now,
thick green curly hair that hangs over brow
'you're being watched', sunk into shades of time
cold stone lips echoing deep chamber fine

paws become talons seeping into mud and stone
and walls closing in like a book spines' bone
as deeper artery gushes pungent bright greens
I stumble out of those remedy sheens

Caving Games are always hard to explain…. >>

Frog's fate

    My love!
        Draw me my sump!
and I shall live in it until   soft sand sucks me in..
but to love you unconditionally   would be as hard and as cold
as the water
      I drown in-
          and the rock I slowly hit
             with my skull as I fall   [down]
stone on stone is surely as soft as   [dow-]
the love that bruised my heart for you   [do-]
or the black water that weighs me   [d-]
as it soaks and stumbles through the cracks of time,   [o--]
until it bubbles up and stretches out its hands   [w-]
to touch my aching ribcage from beneath   [n.]

and sand grips further, holding onto my scaly skin, [sinking]

      until I lay in the heart of this cave [within]

Walking through ground

I realised that my feet were always pointing in your direction
and freedom of movement given in my own rhythm
was bound to set me on a straight course to you
since twists and turns that shake my stride
keep your hands wrapped on my waist in comfort

I hold an acre within a bead that sits in my eyes
and my soul nurtures those greens and blacks;
the cliffs I wept upon and the meadows where I lay
the violet of pains and the mustard yellow of joys
that slowed my steps and hastened my journey
but created lavish divinity before setting my hands

The patterns of time have led me to the same destiny:
to be held in your limestone arms for this short while
you tranced me with soft white temptations
when promising a cold hard denial of the rock you are.

Overlooking Kinder

My temptress of darkness

A nightmare walks with me,
and behind me
as I trudge deep under the
broken bridges
and stuffed up streams
until a secret hole is reached

        [Take me in]

        The howl of the trains that run high
          like the water that rumbles below
            both running the same way
              into the heart of the city
                a fresh thick wave joins
           a clean-cut Victorian sewer

where streams dribble down
into a historic monument
that eyes have long but forgotten.

    estranged company is the nightmare of the dark.
        It is trudging through the underbelly
          cautiously staring into the abyss
           and waiting in an empty chamber
             for a moment of silence

A perfect ridge in Cavedale

My funny valentine

If white foam is tainted by muddy rock and debris
as it rides up the cave walls
then you were not meant to dwell, upon your back
but become a philosopher in your final moment
a hero lies in that golden stoic's heart
to take death so gracefully

but there is no life that I would rather save
than when I sat unknowingly gazing in the sky

But gods had a different opinion
not to suck your pretty bones under sump
but set you free   *-by gods they set you free.*
Oh, faceless creature I remember to forget-
I thank the earth that decided to save you
from the calm that we call death
to live in this havoc world and see you again
rife among the greed, reckless and destructive force
perhaps to see that smile
that cuts through evil for -
one moment.

breathing out bubbles

Do not expect the stillness of the air to last forever-
                the dust tapping your face in quiet darkness.
within the rocky suburb of this underground maze
                we are destined to follow until life sinks away
    when the lash of the river
            and stirring of the mist
       leers lividly round those stubborn, lonesome corners
you can sit there and let the water fill up to your nose
        and only you can decide to swim to shallower depths
or perhaps sinking into the dead air before the havoc
     dropping knees and breaking apart: broken sack of oranges
white stringy tendons pulling you down and clawing at the floor
fingering the cold, stagnant chaos
with lanky white fingers as
juices run down the river
orange fades to brown
and before me lies my final drop
.

The water was DEEP!

Back and Forth:

but then you took it out.
It belonged.
It was sitting so pretty
carved by thousands of years
a mystery force,
resting with dullness, it does not belong here!
shine and resonance
millions of years sitting dull under your desk light
take it back in,
to travel back,
is to restore the former glory of a lost stone,
to promise what mother nature intended:

What I want to unhear

If dedication is the mark of a man,
then they see half of a woman.
If I had to try over and over to impress them
then I'd be the mouse in the dumpster, pleading for scraps.

Rumours travel fast and fleeting
that I had conquered what others wouldn't
in the smallest corners of the peak
escaping the stone that holds onto bones.

"remember when you were attractive? We always thought you'd quit."

but long hair or pretty dress did not define
how I felt.
Nor smiles and kindness towards men
make me a slut.
same woman now, short hair, muddied-suit,
and grown with age. cut-off bleach blonde: cut-off the prying eyes.
Finally, women don't see a threat that was never there.

How can I direct a woman underground?
When her peers will pry on her like sharks
and sink jaws in, only to later tell her

she wasn't really *that* tasty.
that she bore too much flesh *not* to be bitten.

and now rots beneath the waves
as she becomes the 'scraps' at the bottom of the barrel.

Stanage Edge Gritstone

Overlooking

Where others see dusty brown trees scattered
I see my name written in the dirt, holding the roots
If you'd just give me more time, my love
and when I die, don't lie me in some cold cardboard box
But under the trees so I can flourish
To see one more summer
And overlook them all on their brightest days

Plato's cave [iiii]

Scrambling up, the mud sank into her fingers, painting under her nails brown. Eyes shut tight as the golden hues waved into mind and seared eyelids shut. Pain, pin pricking all over face, yet arms outstretched. She could feel the velvet blades of grass, wet with the same water she had soaked in for years. Now, they speckled and jumped as she ran her soft hands over them in large sweeps. A tweeting sound dusted her ears in gold. Slowly, the sun warmed against this skin and filled her smile with daisies.

Two moos

The mist begins to clear

Out of breath
I turn around to see
that each step I took was progress
and the ledge I rested on years ago,
was now a meer shadow in the far distance-
squinting my eyes in reflection.
I thrutched up high to get here,
through the deepest pinching holes.
the effort I had put in each step
was a small triumph over my own evil
that solidified my toes into my shoes,
now comfy on my souls.

But here, I rest on what I have built.
overlooking the view of pain, hurt, love, loss, sacrifice
and beauty
carved by each step
all for me to rest peacefully, here
until I am ready to climb once again

Sunlight in a dark room

Kinship of Blue John

It started raining Blue John
when our eyes first met.
I had a hardened heart
but you understood each beat

and you picked up one piece off the ground
as you picked up your own heart before
and gave it straight to me- without thought.

your kind, cold blues made sense from then on.
They slotted between the cold whites I had
so neatly, that they became purple.
the sweet tinges we left each other will never go away

The Surveyer

After years of wondering in the desert of 'no
        can't
                you probably won't
                      I doubt you could'
I unearthed a smile I spied from a mile away, and then he comes along to say:
'let's'   'of course she can'   'she will'   'you did well'
his presence made me feel safer than before I knew of the evils of this world,
a child once again.
but I must grow up over and over,
to return to the dessert.
In an agonising fight for friendship.
A love never to be told,
only to be whispered in the mists of darkness
and as he scans the room
red lazor in hand,
without saying a word
he shows me back to the mirage I so craved
when he rests his eyes upon mine

Oxlow's Sweet Kiss

slow, delicate, decisive, tapping on my thighs
but I, tripping, falling, fumbling mess in foreground
                [with fresh bruises]
him: unbothered; unbroken and yet-
both stable and in love
                     (..with others)
and free
to kiss
slowly
and sit
and wait
to hear the rain within that rocky cathedral
with stemples high above our heads
and deep cuts of stone around us.
and cocooned within I felt
transformation.
in that fragile cave,
those broken caverns,
became a woman,
with quiet confidence slowly chipped in,
knowing my journey would be slow.
slow in the way he pulled my waist further in..
slow in the way I prussicked,
heavily
up
the cavern.
but no shame nor fear had been brought upon me that
day.

because I had chosen the company of those that fed me,
and made me feel calm,

understood,
loved-
not those that fed *on* me-
using my weaknesses as their gain.

Finally, I had healed-

And I was to blame. (in all the best ways)

Happy to be out

the beacon of hope

fresh lead, drilled and dug,
hollowed and surfaced-
whilst green ivy hung over in wait,
to cover the cold, broken entrance

it waited in black for 300 years
for someone to appreciate its faded hues
and pick-axe strikes

in secret, hushed-voiced cavers inside-
they enjoy the final days
before its grand fill-in.
lost;
once again
for eternity,
as a new block of cheap apartments
destroy any hope of exploration of
'worthless' hidden holes

but even then-
the wet paper-straw stemples will
still hold strong through humanity's
demise
and be discovered, once again.

About the Author

Sheffield University and Sookmyung Women's University graduate, Elise has been spending time exploring the Peak District when she can, honing down on her skills as a cave videographer. Her work can be seen extensively in books, television, and is currently very active on Youtube- where she likes to keep up with writing, producing and presenting.

Contact her:

Instagram - elisefreshwaterblizzard
Email – efreshwaterblizzard@gmail.com

www.ingramcontent.com/pod-product-compliance
Lightning Source LLC
LaVergne TN
LVHW051226070526
838200LV00057B/4621